·*Cooking for Today*·

BALTI COOKING

·*Cooking for Today*·

BALTI COOKING

JENNIE BERESFORD

SIENA

A Siena Book
Siena is an imprint of Parragon Books

First published in Great Britain in 1996 by
Parragon Book Service Ltd
Unit 13–17
Avonbridge Trading Estate
Atlantic Road
Avonmouth
Bristol BS11 9QD

ISBN 0-7525-1459-8

Produced by Haldane Mason, London

Printed in Italy

Acknowledgements:
Art Direction: Ron Samuels
Editor: Michael Williams
Series design: Pedro & Frances Prá-Lopez/Kingfisher Design
Page design: Somewhere Creative
Photography and styling: Patrick McLeavey
Home Economist: Jennie Berresford

Photographs on pages 6, 20, 34, 48 and 62 are reproduced by permission of
ZEFA Picture Library (UK) Ltd.

Note:
Cup measurements in this book are for American cups. Tablespoons are assumed to be 15ml.
Unless otherwise stated, milk is assumed to be full-fat, eggs are standard size 2
and pepper is freshly ground black pepper

Contents

❧

CHAPTER ONE

Appetizers

Although appetizers are not usually served in Pakistani homes, there is a great tradition of eating snacks. In any town in northern Pakistan you will find street vendors selling tasty small portions of spicy food.

Most Balti curry houses will serve a selection of appetizers, to cater for the demand in the West. Balti curries make a great first course and some of the recipes would also make tasty snacks to serve at a drinks party. The recipes can be served as main course dishes if you increase the quantities; you can also use any of the main course recipes for appetizers, reducing the quantities.

Appetizers can be served in small Balti pans, which are just smaller versions of the large Balti cooking pan. These small Balti pans are also useful for cooking small quantities of whole spices.

Opposite: *Evening prayers a the entrance to the Great Mosque at Lahore in Pakista*

STEP 1

STEP 2

STEP 3

STEP 4

BALTI KING PRAWNS (JUMBO SHRIMP)

Although prawns (shrimp) are not a traditional ingredient of Balti cooking, they work well with Balti spices and Balti cooking methods.

SERVES 4
PREPARATION: 10 MINS,
  MARINATING: 2 HRS,
  COOKING: 15 MINS

1 garlic clove, crushed
2 tsp freshly grated ginger root
2 tsp ground coriander
2 tsp ground cumin
$\frac{1}{2}$ tsp ground cardamom
$\frac{1}{4}$ tsp chilli powder
2 tbsp tomato purée (paste)
5 tbsp water
3 tbsp chopped fresh coriander (cilantro)
500 g/1 lb peeled cooked king prawns
  (jumbo shrimp)
2 tbsp oil
2 small onions, sliced
1 fresh green chilli, chopped
salt

1 Put the garlic, ginger, ground coriander, cumin, cardamom, chilli powder, tomato purée (paste), 4 tablespoons of the water and 2 tablespoons of the fresh coriander (cilantro) into a bowl. Mix all the ingredients together.

2 Add the prawns (shrimp) to the bowl and leave to marinate for 2 hours.

3 Heat the oil in a Balti pan or wok, add the onions and stir-fry until golden brown.

4 Add the prawns (shrimp), marinade and the chilli and stir-fry over a medium heat for 5 minutes. Add the salt, and the remaining tablespoon of water if the mixture is very dry. Stir-fry over a medium heat for a further 5 minutes.

5 Serve immediately with the remaining fresh chopped coriander (cilantro).

PRAWNS (SHRIMP)

Smaller prawns (shrimp) can be substituted for the same weight in king prawns (jumbo shrimp), if wished.

GREEN CHILLI & GALANGAL PRAWNS (SHRIMP)

This is a wonderfully simple dish that would be excellent to serve at a dinner party.

STEP 1

STEP 2

STEP 3

STEP 4

SERVES 4
PREPARATION: 10 MINS,
COOKING: 12–15 MINS

2 tbsp oil
4 garlic cloves, crushed
2.5 cm/1 inch fresh galangal root, grated
500g/1lb peeled cooked king prawns (jumbo shrimp)
2 fresh green chillies, sliced
1 tbsp lemon juice
1 tbsp tomato purée (paste)
180 ml/6 fl oz/³⁄₄ cup coconut milk
³⁄₄ tsp Garam Masala (see page 78)
1 tsp salt
1 tbsp chopped fresh coriander (cilantro)

1 Heat the oil in a Balti pan or wok, add the garlic and galangal and stir-fry until golden brown.

2 Add the prawns (shrimp) and green chillies and stir-fry for 3 minutes.

3 Stir in the lemon juice, tomato purée (paste), coconut milk, garam masala and salt. Simmer for 8–10 minutes until the prawns (shrimp) are cooked.

4 Add the fresh coriander (cilantro) and serve at once.

CHILLIES

Chillies come in many shapes, sizes and degrees of hotness and are usually red or green. I have used mainly fresh green chillies, which are generally milder than red chillies, and most supermarkets now state on the label if the fresh chilli is hot or mild. The seeds are the really fiery part, so make sure you remove them if you like a milder curry. Don't touch your face or eyes while handling fresh chillies, as the juices will burn the skin. Dried red chillies are available whole, crushed or ground. Always wash your hands thoroughly after handling chillies.

GALANGAL

Galangal is related to ginger. The root resembles ginger root, but it has a more peppery taste. It is used chopped or sliced. Galangal will probably only be found in Asian food stores. Ginger root can be used as a substitute.

STEP 1

STEP 2

STEP 3

STEP 4

DEEP-FRIED BATTERED FISH WITH FENUGREEK DIP

The crispy, spicy battered fish is complemented by a tangy fenugreek dip. The dish makes a delicious and light start to a meal. Fresh coriander (cilantro) or mint can be substituted for the fenugreek.

SERVES 4
PREPARATION: 15 MINS,
    COOKING 12–16 MINS

125 g/4 oz/1 cup gram flour or plain (all-
    purpose) flour
2 tsp Garam Masala (see page 78)
4 tsp brown mustard seeds
2 eggs
1 tbsp oil
120–150 ml/4–5 fl oz/$^1/_2$–$^2/_3$ cup coconut
    milk
500 g/1 lb plaice fillets, skinned, and cut
    into 1.5 cm/$^5/_8$ inch strips
300 ml/$^1/_2$ pint/1$^1/_4$ cups oil for deep-frying
lemon wedges to serve

DIP:
150 ml/$^1/_4$pint/$^2/_3$ cup thick creamy yogurt
2 tbsp chopped fresh fenugreek
$^1/_2$ tsp Garam Masala (see page 78)
1 tsp tomato purée (paste)

1 Sift the flour into a bowl and add the garam masala and mustard seeds. Make a well in the centre and gradually add the eggs, 1 tablespoon of oil and enough coconut milk to make a batter which has the consistency of thick cream.

2 Coat the fish in the batter and set aside.

3 To make the dip, put the yogurt, fenugreek, garam masala and tomato purée (paste) into a bowl and mix together.

4 Heat the oil in a Balti pan or wok. Add the fish in batches so the pan is not crowded, and deep-fry for 3–4 minutes until golden brown. Transfer the fish on to paper towels to drain then keep warm in a low oven while you cook the rest of the fish.

5 Serve the fish hot with lemon wedges and the dip.

FENUGREEK

Fenugreek is sold in bunches similar to coriander. The stalks should be discarded, as they are very bitter.

SPICED CHICKEN KOFTAS WITH LIME PICKLE

Koftas are spicy meat balls. In this recipe they are made with chicken, but you could use lamb or beef. Lime pickle is available in Asian food stores and some supermarkets.

STEP 1

S ERVES 4
P REPARATION: **15 MINS**,
   C OOKING: **10–20 MINS**

500 g/ 1lb skinned and boned chicken,
  chopped coarsely
1 garlic clove
2.5 cm/ 1 inch piece ginger root, grated
4 tsp Garam Masala (see page 78)
$^1\!/_2$ tsp ground turmeric
2 tbsp chopped fresh coriander (cilantro)
$^1\!/_2$ green (bell) pepper, chopped coarsely
2 fresh green chillies, deseeded
$^1\!/_2$ tsp salt
6 tbsp oil
1 jar lime pickle to serve
lime wedges to garnish

1 Put all the ingredients except the oil and lime pickle into a food processor or blender and process until the mixture is chopped finely. Alternatively, finely chop the chicken, garlic, ginger, (bell) pepper and chillies, and mix together in a bowl with the garam masala, turmeric, coriander (cilantro) and salt.

2 Shape the mixture into 16 small balls.

3 Heat the oil in a Balti pan or wok and fry the koftas for 8–10 minutes, turning them occasionally to ensure they cook evenly. If you cannot fit all the koftas into the pan at once, keep the first batch warm in a low oven, while you fry the remaining koftas.

4 Drain the koftas on paper towels and serve hot with lime pickle.

VEGETARIAN KOFTAS

You could make these into vegetarian koftas by substituting the chicken with 500 g/1 lb of mixed vegetables, such as potatoes, carrots or pumkin. Add the vegetables in place of the chicken in step 1 with 1 egg to bind the ingredients together.

ACCOMPANIMENTS

Instead of lime pickle you could serve Fenugreek Dip (see page 12) or a selection of mango chutney, lime pickle and fenugreek dip.

STEP 2

STEP 3

STEP 4

STEP 1

STEP 2

STEP 3

STEP 4

BALTI MUSHROOM PANEER

A great variety of mushrooms and fungi grow wild in northern Pakistan. Supermarkets now sell quite a lot of different mushrooms, and I have used a mixture for this recipe.

SERVES 4
PREPARATION: 15 MINS,
COOKING: 10–12 MINS

2 tbsp oil
2 small onions, sliced
2 tsp brown mustard seeds
1 garlic clove, crushed
2.5 cm/1 inch piece ginger root, grated
$^1/_2$ tsp chilli powder
500 g/1lb mixed mushrooms, such as oyster, shiitake, brown cap (crimini), and flat
125 g/4 oz paneer, cut into 1 cm/$^1/_2$ inch cubes
150 ml/$^1/_4$ pint/$^2/_3$ cup Balti Sauce (see page 78) or chicken stock
$^1/_4$ tsp salt
2 tsp Garam Masala (see page 78)
1 tbsp chopped fresh coriander (cilantro)

1 Heat the oil in a Balti pan or wok. Add the onions and mustard seeds and fry until the onions have softened.

2 Stir in the garlic, ginger and chilli powder and stir-fry for 1 minute.

3 Add the mushrooms and paneer and stir-fry for 2 minutes.

4 Stir in the Balti sauce or stock, the salt and garam masala and simmer for 5–7 minutes.

5 Stir in the chopped coriander (cilantro) and serve.

PANEER

Paneer is the traditional homemade fresh cheese of Pakistan and India and can be bought in Asian stores. Tofu (bean curd) can be used as a substitute.

To make your own paneer is very simple and quick. Bring to the boil 1.2 litres/2 pints/5 cups of milk, add 3 tbsp of vinegar (any type) or lemon juice, and stir until the milk separates. Strain the curds through a clean piece of muslin (cheesecloth) or tea towel (dish towel). Flatten the paneer on to a plate and put another plate on top with a weight on to force out the liquid. Leave overnight. Use as required.

STEP 1

STEP 2

STEP 3

STEP 4

MINTY LAMB KEBABS WITH CUCUMBER & YOGURT

Yogurt, whether made from cow's milk, ewe's milk or yak's milk, is an important ingredient in Pakistani cooking. It is used either in cooked dishes or served as a side dish.

SERVES 4
PREPARATION: 20 MINS,
  COOKING: 15–20 MINS

2 tsp coriander seeds
2 tsp cumin seeds
3 cloves
3 green cardamom pods
6 black peppercorns
1 cm/^{1}/$_2$ inch piece ginger root
2 garlic cloves
2 tbsp chopped fresh mint
1 small onion, chopped
425 g/14 oz/1^3/$_4$ cups minced (ground)
  lamb
^{1}/$_2$ tsp salt
lime slices to serve

DIP:
150 ml/5 fl oz/^{2}/$_3$ cup natural yogurt
2 tbsp chopped fresh mint
7 cm/3 inch piece of cucumber, grated
1 tsp mango chutney

1 Dry-fry the coriander, cumin, cloves, cardamom pods and peppercorns until they turn a shade darker and release a roasted aroma.

2 Grind the roasted spices in a coffee grinder, spice mill or a pestle and mortar.

3 Put the ginger and garlic into a food processor or blender and process to a purée. Add the ground spices, mint, onion, lamb and salt and process until chopped finely. Alternatively, finely chop the garlic and ginger and mix with the ground spices and remaining kebab ingredients.

4 Mould the kebab mixture into small sausage shapes on 4 kebab skewers. Cook under a preheated hot grill (broiler) for 10–15 minutes, turning the skewers occasionally.

5 To make the dip, mix together the ingredients.

6 Serve the kebabs with lime slices and the dip.

TIPS

The kebabs are ideal for cooking on a barbecue in the summer.
  Instead of roasting and grinding the spices, use 2 teaspoons of Garam Masala (see page 78).

18

CHAPTER TWO

Poultry & Game

Chicken is probably the most frequently used meat in Balti cooking; as it does not take too long to cook it lends itself well to the quick stir-fry cooking method. You can either buy whole chickens and joint them yourself, or buy chicken pieces, or, for convenience, use boneless chicken breasts. The chickens used in Pakistan are free-range and scrawny, but as I have experienced in many Asian countries, they taste far better than our battery-reared birds. Marinating the chicken really helps to give it a more interesting flavour.

Pakistan has a great variety of game birds which are very popular to eat. The most regularly eaten is quail. Quail is readily available in most supermarkets and butchers.

Opposite: *The Kaghan Valley in northern Pakistan.*

STEP 2

STEP 3

STEP 4

STEP 5

TRADITIONAL BALTI CHICKEN

Most families in Pakistan keep some domestic chickens for egg production and eating. This recipe uses tomatoes, onions, spices and fresh coriander (cilantro), which form the basis of many Balti sauces.

SERVES 4
PREPARATION: 15 MINS,
    COOKING: 30–35 MINS

3 tbsp oil
4 green cardamom pods
2 tsp cumin seeds
2 onions, sliced
2 garlic cloves, crushed
1.25 kg/2¹/₂ lb chicken, skinned and jointed into 8 pieces, or 8 small chicken portions
1 tsp chilli powder
¹/₂ tsp salt
1 tsp Garam Masala (see page 78)
90 ml/3¹/₂ fl oz/6 tbsp water
10 tomatoes, chopped coarsely
2 tbsp chopped fresh coriander (cilantro)

1 Heat the oil in a Balti pan or wok, add the cardamom pods and cumin seeds and fry until the seeds pop.

2 Stir in the onions and garlic and fry until golden brown.

3 Add the chicken and stir-fry for 5–6 minutes until brown.

4 Stir in the chilli powder, salt, garam masala, water and tomatoes. Bring to the boil, then turn the heat down and simmer for 20–25 minutes, until the chicken juices run clear when the thickest parts of the pieces are pierced with a sharp knife. Turn the chicken over halfway through cooking.

5 Stir in the coriander (cilantro) and serve at once.

LEFTOVER CHICKEN

You could use leftover chicken in this recipe, but instead of stir-frying it, add it when you add the tomatoes.

VARIATIONS

The traditional Balti chicken recipe is a good basis for trying out your own combination of ingredients to make your own original curry. At step 4 you could add: par-cooked diced vegetables such as okra, aubergine, potato, (bell) pepper, etc. Pulses could also be used – add a 425 g/ 14 oz can of beans or lentils with the vegetables at step 4. You could also try using different whole spices, to see which flavours you prefer.

STEP 1

STEP 2

STEP 3

STEP 4

CHICKEN, CORIANDER (CILANTRO), GINGER & LEMON STIR-FRY

The sweet and sour flavours in this recipe reflect the influence of neighbouring China.

SERVES 4
PREPARATION: 15 MINS,
  COOKING: 20–25 MINS

3 tbsp oil
750 g/ 1½ lb chicken breast, skinned, boned
  and cut in 5 cm/ 2 inch strips
3 garlic cloves, crushed
3.5 cm/ 1½ inch piece ginger root, cut into
  strips
1 tsp pomegranate seeds, crushed
½ tsp ground turmeric
1 tsp Garam Masala (see page 78)
2 fresh green chillies, sliced
½ tsp salt
4 tbsp lemon juice
grated rind of 1 lemon
6 tbsp chopped fresh coriander (cilantro)
120 ml/ 4 fl oz/ ½ cup chicken stock

1 Heat the oil in a Balti pan or wok and stir-fry the chicken until golden brown on both sides. Remove the chicken from the pan and set aside.

2 Fry the garlic, ginger and pomegranate seeds in the oil for 1 minute.

3 Stir in the turmeric, garam masala and chillies and fry for 30 seconds.

4 Return the chicken to the pan and add the salt, lemon juice, lemon rind, coriander (cilantro) and stock. Stir the chicken to ensure it is coated in the sauce. Bring to the boil, then lower the heat and simmer for 10–15 minutes until the chicken juices run clear when the thickest part of the chicken is pierced with a sharp knife.

5 Serve with naan bread or aromatic basmatic rice (see page 74).

SUMMER DISH

This dish can be served cold in the summer with a spicy rice salad or a mixed lettuce salad.

STEP 1

STEP 2

STEP 3

STEP 4

BALTI CHICKEN PANEER

This recipe is based on one of the most popular Balti recipes, Balti chicken in butter sauce. The poppy seeds in the sauce enhance the nutty taste of the almonds.

SERVES 4
PREPARATION: 20 MINS,
    COOKING: 25–30 MINS

60 g/2 oz/$^{1}/_{2}$ cup ground almonds
250 g/8 oz/1 cup chopped tomatoes
2 fresh green chillies, chopped
1 tsp poppy seeds
1 garlic clove
150 ml/$^{1}/_{4}$ pint/$^{2}/_{3}$ cup natural yogurt
90 g/3 oz/$^{2}/_{3}$ cup butter
750 g/1$^{1}/_{2}$lb chicken breast meat, cut into
    2.5 cm/1 inch cubes
175 g/6 oz paneer (see page 16), cut into
    1 cm/$^{1}/_{2}$ inch cubes
1 tsp ground cumin
1 tsp paprika
1 tsp Garam Masala (see page 78)
$^{1}/_{4}$ tsp ground cinnamon
$^{1}/_{2}$ tsp salt

TO GARNISH:
1 tbsp chopped fresh coriander (cilantro)
30 g/1 oz/$^{1}/_{4}$ cup flaked slivered almonds,
    toasted

1 Put the ground almonds, tomatoes, chillies, poppy seeds and garlic in a food processor or blender and blend to a smooth paste. Alternatively, push the tomatoes through a sieve (strainer), finely chop the chillies and garlic, crush the poppy seeds, then mix together the tomatoes, chillies, garlic, poppy seeds and ground almonds. Stir the yogurt into the tomato mixture.

2 Heat the butter in a Balti pan or wok, add the chicken and stir-fry for 5 minutes.

3 Add the paneer, cumin, paprika, garam masala, cinnamon and salt and stir-fry for 1 minute.

4 Slowly add the tomato and yogurt mixture to prevent the yogurt curdling. Simmer for 10–15 minutes until the chicken juices run clear when the chicken is pierced with a sharp knife.

5 Serve garnished with the coriander (cilantro) and flaked almonds.

TIPS

A 1.25 kg/2½ lb chicken on the bone could be used, but you will have to cook the dish for longer depending on the size of the chicken pieces; for example, a leg will have to be simmered for 30–35 minutes. To make the sauce really rich you could add a couple of tablespoons of cream during the final stage of cooking.

CHICKEN & BLACK-EYE BEANS (PEAS)

Pulses are a valuable source of nourishment in cold mountainous areas in the winter months, when meat is scarce. You could use any variety of pulses in this recipe, but adjust the cooking times accordingly.

STEP 1

SERVES 4
PREPARATION: 15 MINS,
  SOAKING: OVERNIGHT,
  COOKING: 45 MINS

250 g/8 oz/1 generous cup dried black-eye beans (peas), soaked overnight and drained
1 tsp salt
2 onions, chopped
2 garlic cloves, crushed
1 tsp ground turmeric
1 tsp ground cumin
1.25 kg/2½ lb chicken, jointed into 8 pieces
1 green (bell) pepper, chopped
2 tbsp oil
2.5 cm/1 inch piece ginger root, grated
2 tsp coriander seeds
½ tsp fennel seeds
2 tsp Garam Masala (see page 78)
1 tbsp chopped fresh coriander (cilantro) to garnish

1 Put the beans into a Balti pan, wok or saucepan with the salt, onions, garlic, turmeric and cumin. Cover the beans with water, bring to the boil and cook for 15 minutes.

2 Add the chicken and green (bell) pepper to the pan and bring to the boil. Lower the heat and simmer gently

for 30 minutes until the beans are tender and the chicken juices run clear when the thickest parts of the pieces are pierced with a sharp knife.

3 Heat the oil in a Balti pan, wok or frying pan (skillet) and fry the ginger, coriander seeds and fennel seeds for 30 seconds.

4 Stir the ginger, coriander seeds and fennel seeds into the chicken and add the garam masala. Simmer for a further 5 minutes and serve garnished with fresh coriander (cilantro).

STEP 2

STEP 3

CANNED BEANS

For convenience, use 425 g/14 oz can of black-eye beans (peas) instead of dried beans (peas). Add at step 2.

STEP 4

BALTI QUAIL

Quail has been part of the diet in northern Pakistan throughout the years; in fact game birds of any sort are very popular. The 'gamey' taste of Quail is complemented deliciously by the spices used in Balti cooking.

STEP 1

STEP 2

STEP 4

STEP 6

SERVES 4
PREPARATION: 15 MINS,
   MARINATING: 2 HRS,
   COOKING: 35 MINS

4 quail, roughly jointed
1.5 cm/²/₃ inch piece ginger root, grated
2 garlic cloves, crushed
1 tsp ground cumin
2 tsp Garam Masala (see page 78)
2 tsp paprika
1 tsp ground turmeric
1 tbsp chopped fresh mint
²/₃ tsp salt
250 ml/8 fl oz/1 cup natural yogurt
2 tbsp oil
8 baby onions, total weight about
   250 g/8 oz
4 courgettes (zucchini), sliced thickly
1 fresh green chilli, chopped
4 lime wedges to garnish

1 Using a sharp knife, make cuts in several places in the skin and flesh of each quail joint.

2 Mix together the ginger, garlic, cumin, garam masala, paprika, turmeric, mint, salt and yogurt. Add the quail and coat in the sauce.

3 Cover and leave in the refrigerator to marinate for 2 hours or overnight.

4 Put the quail on a rack over a roasting tin (pan) containing about 2.5 cm/1 inch depth of water; this keeps the quail moist during cooking. Roast the quail in a preheated oven at 200°C/ 400°F/ Gas mark 6 for 30 minutes, until the quail juices run clear when the thickest part of each piece is pierced with a sharp knife.

5 Heat the oil in a Balti pan or wok and fry the onions, courgettes (zucchini) and chilli for 5–6 minutes until golden brown and tender.

6 Add the cooked quail to the pan and serve with lime wedges.

VARIATION

Baby chicken or chicken joints can be used instead of quail.

SWEET & SOUR BALTI DUCK

The sweet and sour flavours that are often used in Balti cooking were introduced by the Chinese traders who passed between the two countries.

STEP 1

STEP 2

STEP 3

STEP 4

SERVES 4
PREPARATION: 10 MINS,
   COOKING: 25–30 MINS

4 tbsp oil
¹/₂ tsp cumin seeds
¹/₂ tsp brown mustard seeds
¹/₂ tsp crushed dried pomegranate seeds
1 onion, sliced
1 garlic clove, chopped
1 cm/¹/₂ inch piece ginger root, shredded
2 fresh green chillies, sliced
4 duck breasts, boned and sliced into 5 cm/
   2 inch strips
¹/₂ tsp salt
150 ml/¹/₄ pint /²/₃ cup orange juice
1 orange, quartered and sliced
2 tsp ground turmeric
¹/₂ tsp Garam Masala (see page 78)
1 tbsp white wine vinegar
shredded orange rind to garnish

1 Heat the oil in a Balti pan or wok and fry the cumin seeds, mustard seeds and pomegranate seeds until they start popping.

2 Add the onion, garlic, ginger and chillies and stir-fry until the onions are golden brown.

3 Add the duck and stir-fry for 5 minutes until it is brown on both sides.

4 Stir in the salt, orange juice, orange slices, turmeric, garam masala and vinegar and bring to the boil. Lower the hear and simmer for 15–20 minutes until the duck is tender but still pinkish inside; if you prefer duck to be well done, cook for longer. Serve garnished with shredded orange rind.

POMEGRANATE SEEDS

Dried pomegranate seeds can be bought at Asian stores and will give a very individual tangy taste. Alternatively, you could use the seeds from the fresh fruit.

CHAPTER THREE

Meat

The most commonly eaten meats in northern Pakistan are mutton and goat. I have used lamb instead of mutton, as it is more tender and cooks more quickly. Mutton has a stronger taste but requires hours of slow cooking, and is not as widely available as lamb. Lamb can readily be bought diced or minced (ground) from butchers and supermarkets. Goat can be found in specialist halal butchers or some Asian food stores. If you use goat instead of lamb in a recipe, it will take longer to cook. Pork is never found on the menu because Pakistan is a Muslim country; for the same reason traditionally no alcohol is served with a meal.

The meat will nearly always be par-cooked to save time in the final cooking. Meat dishes will often incorporate vegetables to make a complete meal in one pan. This type of dish is ideal when cooking a quick evening meal, as you only need to serve naan bread or chapatis to accompany it; it also saves on washing up. For a special meal serve one or two Balti curries with a vegetable dish, pulse dish and naan bread.

Opposite: *A flock of sheep grazing high in the Hunza mountains of Northern Pakistan .*

STEP 2

STEP 3

STEP 4

STEP 5

PATHAN BEEF STIR-FRY

Unlike some parts of neighbouring India where it is forbidden by the Hindu religion, beef is eaten in Pakistan. However, it is not as popular as lamb, goat or chicken.

SERVES 4
PREPARATION: 15 MINS,
  MARINATING: 1–2 HRS,
  COOKING: 15–20 MINS

750 g/1¹/₂ lb fillet of beef, cut into 2.5 cm/
  1 inch strips
2 tbsp oil
1 onion
2.5 cm/1 inch piece ginger root, cut into
  strips
1 fresh red chilli, deseeded and sliced
2 carrots, cut into strips
1 green (bell) pepper, cut into strips
1 tsp Garam Masala (see page 78)
1 tbsp toasted sesame seeds

MARINADE:
1 tsp dried fenugreek
1 tsp brown mustard seeds, ground
1 tsp ground cinnamon
1 tsp ground cumin
1 garlic clove, crushed
150 ml/¹/₄ pint/²/₃ cup natural yogurt

1 To make the marinade, mix all the marinade ingredients in a bowl.

2 Add the beef to the marinade, stir to coat, then cover and leave to marinate for 1–2 hour, or overnight in the refrigerator.

3 Heat the oil in a Balti pan or wok, add the onion and stir-fry until softened.

4 Stir in the ginger, chilli, carrots and green (bell) pepper and stir-fry for 1 minute. Add the garam masala and beef with the marinade liquids, and stir-fry for 8–10 minutes until the beef is tender; it is best if it is still pinkish inside.

5 Stir in the toasted sesame seeds and serve.

VARIATIONS

Any selection of vegetables can be added to the stir-fry, which is a good way to use up any vegetables left over in the refrigerator, but add them to the beef for just long enough to heat through.

TAMARIND BEEF BALTI

Tamarind has been used in Asian cooking for centuries and gives a sour fruity flavour to the sauce.

STEP 2

STEP 3

STEP 4

STEP 5

SERVES 4
PREPARATION: 15 MINS,
 SOAKING: OVERNIGHT,
 COOKING: 25–30 MINS

125 g/4 oz tamarind block, broken into
 pieces
150 ml/¼ pint/⅔ cup water
2 tbsp tomato purée (paste)
1 tbsp granulated sugar
2.5 cm/1 inch piece ginger root, chopped
1 garlic clove, chopped
½ tsp salt
1 onion, chopped
2 tbsp oil
1 tsp cumin seeds
1 tsp coriander seeds
1 tsp brown mustard seeds
4 curry leaves
750 g/1½ lb braising steak, cut into
 2.5 cm/1 inch cubes and par-cooked (see
 page 78)
1 red (bell) pepper, cut in half, sliced
2 fresh green chillies, deseeded, sliced
1 tsp Garam Masala (see page 78)
1 tbsp chopped fresh coriander (cilantro) to
 garnish

1 Soak the tamarind overnight in the water. Strain the soaked tamarind, keeping the liquid.

2 Put the tamarind, tomato purée (paste), sugar, ginger, garlic, salt and onion into a food processor or blender and mix to a smooth purée. Alternatively, mash the ingredients together in a bowl.

3 Heat the oil in a Balti pan or wok, add the cumin, coriander seeds, mustard seeds and curry leaves, and cook until the spices start popping.

4 Stir the beef into the spices and stir-fry for 2–4 minutes until the meat is browned.

5 Add the red (bell) pepper, chillies, garam masala, tamarind mixture and reserved tamarind liquid and cook for 20–25 minutes. Serve garnished with fresh coriander (cilantro).

SUBSTITUTES

Bay leaves can be substituted for the curry leaves, although they will not give quite the same spicy taste. Instead of tamarind you could use 4 tablespoons of lemon juice.

LAMB KOFTAS WITH SPINACH & CARDAMOM

I have used fresh spinach, but you could use 250 g/8 oz frozen spinach.
The cardamom and nutmeg bring out the sweet flavour of the lamb.

STEP 1

SERVES 4
PREPARATION: 15 MINS,
   COOKING: 45 MINS

5 tbsp oil
2 tsp cardamom seeds
6 black peppercorns, crushed
1 tsp cumin seeds
1 onion, chopped finely
1 garlic clove, crushed
150 ml/¼ pint/⅔ cup natural yogurt
500 g/1 lb chopped fresh spinach
½ tsp grated nutmeg
1 tsp Garam Masala (see page 78)
1 tsp salt
90 g/3 oz/¾ cup split almonds, shredded

KOFTAS:
1 onion, quartered
1 garlic clove
1 fresh green chilli, deseeded
1 tsp Garam Masala (see page 78)
1 tsp salt
750 g/1½ lb minced/3 cups (ground) lamb

1 To make the koftas, put the onion, garlic and chilli into a food processor or blender and process until chopped finely, then add the garam masala, salt and lamb and process to combine the ingredients. Alternatively, finely chop the onion, garlic and chilli,

then mix with the garam masala, salt and lamb in a bowl.

2 Shape the lamb mixture into small balls. Heat 3 tablespoons of the oil in a Balti pan or wok, add the koftas in batches and cook, turning frequently, until evenly browned. Remove the koftas from the pan with a perforated spoon, drain on paper towels and keep warm.

STEP 2

3 Heat the remaining oil in the pan and fry the cardamom seeds, peppercorns and cumin seeds until they start popping. Add the onion and garlic and cook until golden brown.

4 Gradually add the yogurt, stirring all the time to prevent it curdling. Stir in the spinach, nutmeg, garam masala, salt, two-thirds of the almonds and the koftas and simmer for 30 minutes. Sprinkle over the remaining almonds and serve.

STEP 3

VARIATIONS

Instead of lamb, chicken or beef could be used, either as koftas, or as bite-size pieces, which would reduce the preparation time.

STEP 4

BALTI LAMB ROGAN JOSH

Rogan Josh originated in Kashmir at the time of the Moguls. When it is cooked, the lamb is bathed in a rich, red gravy.

STEP 1

STEP 2

STEP 3

STEP 4

SERVES 4
PREPARATION: 10 MINS,
   COOKING: 40 MINS

3 tbsp fennel seeds
1 cm/$^1/_2$ inch piece cinnamon stick
4 black peppercorns
3 tbsp oil
2 onions, sliced
2 garlic cloves, crushed
2.5 cm/1 inch piece ginger root, grated
750 g/1$^1/_2$ lb lamb, cut into 2.5 cm/1 inch
   cubes and par-cooked (see page 78)
8 tomatoes, chopped
1 green (bell) pepper, sliced
150 ml/$^1/_4$pint/$^2/_3$ cup natural yogurt
3 tsp paprika
$^1/_2$ tsp chilli powder
$^1/_2$ tsp Garam Masala (see page 78)
300 ml/$^1/_2$ pint/ 1$^1/_4$ cups Balti Sauce (see
   page 78) or lamb stock

TO GARNISH :
2 tbsp chopped fresh coriander (cilantro)
2 tbsp natural yogurt

1 Grind the fennel seeds, cinnamon and peppercorns to a fine powder in a coffee grinder, spice mill or pestle and mortar.

2 Heat the oil in a Balti pan or wok, add the onions and stir-fry until softened. Add the garlic and ginger and stir-fry for 1 minute.

3 Add the par-cooked lamb, stir-fry for 3 minutes, then add the tomatoes and green (bell) pepper. Stir-fry for 1 minute.

4 Slowly stir in the yogurt, then add the paprika, chilli powder, ground spices, garam masala and Balti sauce or stock. Simmer for 30 minutes until the sauce is reduced to the consistency of a thick gravy.

5 Serve garnished with fresh coriander (cilantro) and yogurt.

T I P

If you don't want to par-cook the lamb, you can start the recipe with raw meat, brown it as the first step of the recipe, then remove it from the pan while you fry the onions and continue with the recipe, adding the meat at Step 4. Cover the pan with foil and cook on the hob or in a preheated oven at 180°C/350°F/Gas mark 4 for 1 hour, until the meat is tender.

MASALA LAMB & LENTILS

*This recipe makes a good warming winter curry. I have used gram
lentils but you could use split yellow peas.*

STEP 1

STEP 3

STEP 4

STEP 5

SERVES 4
PREPARATION: 15 MINS,
  SOAKING: 6 HRS,
  COOKING: 1 HR 15 MINS

2 tbsp oil
1 tsp cumin seeds
2 bay leaves
2.5 cm/1 inch piece cinnamon stick
1 onion, chopped
750 g/1½ lb lean, boneless lamb, cut into
  2.5 cm/1 inch cubes
125 g/4 oz/½ cup split gram lentils, soaked
  for 6 hours and drained
1 tsp salt
1 fresh green chilli, sliced
1.25 litres/2¼ pints/5 cups water
1 garlic clove, crushed
¼ tsp ground turmeric
1 tsp chilli powder
½ tsp Garam Masala (see page 78)
  (optional)
1 tbsp chopped fresh coriander (cilantro)
  (optional)

1 Heat the oil in a Balti pan or wok
and add the cumin seeds, bay
leaves and cinnamon and fry until the
seeds start popping.

2 Add the onion to the pan and stir-
fry until golden brown.

3 Stir the lamb into the onion and
stir-fry until browned.

4 Add the lentils, salt, chilli, water,
garlic, turmeric and chilli powder.
Bring to the boil, then simmer for 1 hour
until the meat and lentils are tender.

5 Taste and stir the garam masala
into the pan, if liked, and cook for a
further 5 minutes. Stir in the coriander
(cilantro), if using, and serve.

TIMESAVER

To save time on soaking, use a 425 g/14 oz
can of lentils. These should be added at
the end of stage 4 and cooked for 15
minutes. The meat still needs the same
cooking time.

STEP 2

STEP 3

STEP 4

STEP 5

BALTI KEEMA WITH SWEET POTATOES, OKRA & SPINACH

Pakistan was influenced not only by China to the east but also by the countries to the west, as can still be seen in the use of ingredients such as sultanas (golden raisins), sugar and nuts in savoury dishes.

SERVES 4
PREPARATION: 10 MINS,
COOKING: 25–30 MINS

250 g/8 oz sweet potatoes, cut into chunks
175 g/6 oz okra
2 tbsp oil
2 onions, sliced
2 garlic cloves, crushed
1 cm/^{1}/$_2$ inch piece ginger root, chopped
500 g/1 lb/2 cups minced (ground) lamb
250 g/8 oz/6 cups fresh spinach, chopped
300 ml/^{1}/$_2$ pint/1^1/$_4$ cups lamb stock
^{1}/$_2$ tsp salt
125 g/4 oz/1 cup pine nuts
125 g/4 oz/^{3}/$_4$ cup sultanas (golden raisins)
1 tbsp granulated sugar
3 tsp Garam Masala (see page 78)
rice or naan bread to serve

1 Bring 2 saucepans of water to the boil. Add the sweet potatoes to one and the okra to the other. Boil both for 4–5 minutes, then drain well. Cut the okra into 1 cm/^{1}/$_2$ inch slices. Set aside both vegetables.

2 Heat the oil in a Balti pan or wok, add the onions and stir-fry until golden brown. Stir in the garlic and ginger and fry for 1 minute.

3 Add the lamb to the pan and stir-fry for 5 minutes.

4 Stir in the sweet potato, okra and spinach and stir-fry for 2 minutes.

5 Add the stock, salt, pine nuts, sultanas (golden raisins), sugar and garam masala and simmer for 10–15 minutes until the sauce has thickened. Serve with rice or naan bread.

ALTERNATIVES

Sweet potato gives a wonderful flavour to the dish, but you could use pumpkin, which has a sweetish taste similar to that of sweet potatoes, or ordinary potatoes.

46

CHAPTER FOUR

Fish & Seafood

Northern Pakistan has no easy access to the sea, but it does have a great many rivers and lakes, so freshwater fish are available. In the winter months the lakes are frozen, so fishing tends to be very seasonal. This is one of the reasons why fish is not used a great deal in Balti cooking. Balti curry houses will only serve a few fish dishes and often fish and meat are mixed together in one dish, although prawns (shrimp) are a popular addition to the menus.

Fish and seafood adapt very well to the Balti method of cooking, and any type of fish can be substituted in the recipes. A fishmonger will clean, fillet and skin the fish for you, which makes it a very convenient main ingredient. Prawns (shrimp) are readily available and can be bought frozen or fresh, unpeeled, or peeled for convenience. Meaty king prawns (jumbo shrimp) are the best choice for a Balti curry recipe.

Opposite: *Fish are found in abundance in the mountain lakes of Kashmir.*

STEP 1

STEP 2

STEP 3

STEP 4

BALTI SCALLOPS WITH CORIANDER (CILANTRO) & TOMATO

This is a wonderful recipe for a special occasion dish. The scallops are succulent with a spicy flavour.

SERVES 4
PREPARATION: 10 MINS,
MARINATING: 1 HR,
COOKING: 10–12 MINS

750 g/ 1¹/₂ lb shelled scallops
2 onions, chopped
3 tomatoes, quartered
2 fresh green chillies, sliced
2 tbsp oil
4 lime wedges to garnish

MARINADE:
3 tbsp chopped fresh coriander (cilantro)
2.5 cm/ 1 inch piece ginger root, grated
1 tsp ground coriander
3 tbsp lemon juice
grated rind of 1 lemon
¹/₄ tsp ground black pepper
¹/₂ tsp salt
¹/₂ tsp ground cumin
1 garlic clove, crushed

1 To make the marinade, mix all the ingredients together in a bowl.

2 Put the scallops into a bowl. Add the marinade and turn the scallops until they are well coated. Then cover and leave to marinate for 1 hour or overnight in the fridge.

3 Heat the oil in a Balti pan or wok, add the onions and stir-fry until softened. Add the tomatoes and chillies and stir-fry for 1 minute.

4 Add the scallops and stir-fry for 6–8 minutes until the scallops are cooked through, but still succulent inside. Serve garnished with lime wedges.

SCALLOPS

It is best to buy the scallops fresh in the shell with the roe – you will need 1.5 kg/ 3 lb – a fishmonger will clean them and remove the shell for you.

STEP 1

STEP 2

STEP 3

STEP 4

KING PRAWNS (JUMBO SHRIMP) WITH SPICED COURGETTES (ZUCCHINI)

King prawns (jumbo shrimp) are meaty so take up the flavour of the spices well, but you could use smaller prawns (shrimp) instead.

SERVES 4
PREPARATION: 10 MINS,
   COOKING: 15 MINS

3 tbsp oil
2 onion, chopped
3 garlic cloves, chopped
1 cm/^{1}/$_2$ inch piece ginger root, chopped
250 g/8 oz courgettes (zucchini), sliced
1 tsp dried pomegranate seeds, crushed
8 tomatoes, chopped
1 tbsp tomato purée (paste)
150 ml/^{1}/$_4$ pint/^{2}/$_3$ cup coconut milk
2 tbsp chopped fresh coriander (cilantro)
1 tsp chilli powder
1 tsp ground cumin
^{1}/$_2$ tsp salt
500 g/1 lb peeled cooked king prawns
   (jumbo shrimp)
fresh coriander (cilantro) to garnish
naan bread, to serve

1 Heat the oil in a Balti pan or wok, add the onions and stir-fry until golden brown. Add the garlic and ginger and stir-fry for 1 minute.

2 Stir the courgettes (zucchini) and pomegranate seeds into the pan and stir-fry for 2 minutes.

3 Add the tomatoes, tomato purée (paste), coconut milk, fresh coriander (cilantro), chilli powder, cumin and salt and stir-fry for a further 2 minutes.

4 Stir in the prawns, bring to the boil then simmer for 6 minutes. Garnish with fresh coriander (cilantro) and serve with naan bread.

ADDING SPICE

If you want a more spicy dish, add more chilli powder or 2 teaspoons Garam Masala (see page 78).

VARIATION

This recipe works well with lobster, monkfish or scallops, instead of king prawns (jumbo prawns). The scallops and lobster should be cooked for only 3 minutes.

BALTI COD & RED LENTILS

The aniseed used in this recipe gives a very delicate aroma to the fish and really enhances the flavour. Instead of serving with the usual naan bread and chapatis, try serving warm wholemeal (whole wheat) bread.

STEP 1

STEP 2

STEP 3

STEP 4

SERVES 4
PREPARATION: 10 MINS,
   COOKING: 56 MINS

2 tbsp oil
$^1/_4$ tsp ground asafoetida (optional)
1 tbsp crushed aniseed
1 tsp ground ginger
1 tsp chilli powder
$^1/_4$ tsp ground turmeric
250 g/8 oz/1 cup split red lentils, washed
1 tsp salt
500 g/1 lb cod, skinned, filleted and cut into
   2.5 cm/1 inch cubes
1 fresh red chilli, chopped
3 tbsp natural yogurt
2 tbsp chopped fresh coriander (cilantro)

1 Heat the oil in a Balti pan or wok, add the asafoetida, if using, and fry for about 10 seconds to burn off the smell of the asafoetida. Add the aniseed, ginger, chilli powder and turmeric and fry for 30 seconds.

2 Stir in the lentils and salt and add enough water to cover the lentils. Bring to the boil, then simmer gently for 45 minutes, until the lentils are soft but not mushy.

3 Add the cod and chilli, bring to the boil and simmer for a further 10 minutes.

4 Stir in the yogurt and fresh coriander (cilantro) and serve straight away.

ASAFOETIDA

Asafoetida is a digestive, so will help in the digestion of the lentils.

Ground asafoetida is easier to use than the type that comes on a block. It should only be used in small quantities. Do not be put off by the smell which is very pungent.

STEP 1

STEP 2

STEP 3

STEP 4

CREAMY FISH & PRAWN (SHRIMP) MASALA

Garam masala (see page 78) is the real essence of Balti cooking. For this reason it is important to use freshly roasted and ground garam masala, as it gives a more subtle flavour.

SERVES 4
PREPARATION: 10 MINS,
  MARINATING: 1 HR,
  COOKING: 15–20 MINS

1 tsp ground coriander
250 ml/8 fl oz/1 cup natural yogurt
1 tsp ground turmeric
1 tsp salt
500 g/1 lb firm white fish such as cod or
  haddock, skinned, filleted and cut into
  2.5 cm/1 inch cubes
250 g/8 oz/¼ cup peeled cooked king
  prawns (jumbo shrimp)
2 tbsp oil
1 tsp brown mustard seeds
1 onion, chopped
1 garlic clove, crushed
2 tsp Garam Masala (see page 78)
2 tbsp chopped fresh coriander (cilantro)
120 ml/4 fl oz/½ cup double (heavy) cream

TO GARNISH:
1 tbsp crushed dried red chillies
sprigs of fresh coriander (cilantro)

1 Put the ground coriander, yogurt, turmeric and salt into a bowl and stir together. Add the fish and prawns (shrimp) and leave to marinate for 1 hour.

2 Heat the oil in a Balti pan or wok, add the mustard seeds and fry until they start popping.

3 Add the onion to the pan, stir-fry until golden brown, then add the garlic and stir-fry for 1 minute.

4 Stir in the garam masala, fresh coriander (cilantro), marinated fish and prawns (shrimp). Simmer for 10–15 minutes until the fish flakes easily when tested with a fork. Stir in the cream during the last few minutes of cooking.

5 Serve garnished with crushed red chillies and fresh coriander (cilantro) sprig.

FISH

Any type of white fish, or smoked haddock or cod, can be used in this recipe.

DELICATELY SPICED TROUT

The mountains of Pakistan feed many lakes and rivers, including the River Indus. Fresh trout are found in the rivers that are in flow throughout the year in the mountainous areas.

STEP 1

SERVES 4
PREPARATION: 10 MINS,
  MARINATING: 30–40 MINS,
  COOKING: 20 MINS

4 trout, each weighing 175–250 g/6–8 oz, cleaned
3 tbsp oil
1 tsp fennel seeds
1tsp onion seeds
1 garlic clove, crushed
150 ml/¼ pint/⅔ cup coconut milk or fish stock
3 tbsp tomato purée (paste)
60 g/2 oz/⅓ cup sultanas (golden raisins)
½ tsp Garam Masala (see page 78)

TO GARNISH:
30 g/ 1 oz/¼ cup chopped cashew nuts
lemon wedges
sprigs of fresh coriander (cilantro)

MARINADE:
4 tbsp lemon juice
2 tbsp chopped fresh coriander (cilantro)
1 tsp ground cumin
½ tsp salt
½ tsp ground black pepper

1 Slash the trout skin in several places on both sides to ensure the marinade is absorbed into the fish faster.

2 To make the marinade, mix all the ingredients together in a bowl.

3 Put the trout in a shallow dish and pour over the marinade. Leave to marinate for 30–40 minutes; turn the fish over during the marinating time.

4 Heat the oil in a Balti pan or wok and fry the fennel seeds and onion seeds until they start popping. Add the garlic, coconut milk or fish stock, and tomato purée (paste) and bring to the boil.

5 Add the sultanas (golden raisins), garam masala and trout with the juices from the marinade. Cover the pan with foil and simmer for 5 minutes. Turn the trout over carefully and simmer for a further 10 minutes. Serve garnished with cashew nuts, lemon wedges and coriander (cilantro) sprigs.

SULTANAS (GOLDEN RAISINS)

Sultanas (golden raisins) add a sweet taste to the sauce, but if you do not like the combination, leave them out.

STEP 3

STEP 4

STEP 5

MONKFISH & OKRA BALTI

In Pakistan okra is known as bindi, and you may also know it by the name of ladies' fingers. Okra can be found both in supermarkets and Asian food stores.

STEP 2

STEP 4

STEP 5

STEP 6

SERVES 4
PREPARATION: 15 MINS,
   MARINATING: 1 HR,
   COOKING: 22 MINS

750 g/1½ lb monkfish, cut into 3 cm/
   1¼ inch cubes
250 g/8 oz okra
2 tbsp oil
1 onion, sliced
1 garlic clove, crushed
2.5 cm/1 inch piece ginger root, sliced
150 ml/¼ pint/⅔ cup coconut milk or fish
   stock
2 tsp Garam Masala (see page 78)

MARINADE:
3 tbsp lemon juice
grated rind of 1 lemon
¼ tsp aniseed
½ tsp salt
½ tsp ground black pepper

TO GARNISH:
4 lime wedges
sprigs of fresh coriander (cilantro)

1 To make the marinade, mix the ingredients together in a bowl.

2 Stir the monkfish into the bowl and leave to marinate for 1 hour.

3 Bring a large saucepan of water to the boil, add the okra and boil for 4–5 minutes. Drain well and cut into 1 cm/½ inch slices.

4 Heat the oil in a Balti pan or wok, add the onion and stir-fry until golden brown. Add the garlic and ginger and fry for 1 minute.

5 Add the fish with the marinade juices to the pan and stir-fry for 2 minutes.

6 Stir in the okra, coconut milk or stock, and the garam masala and simmer for 10 minutes. Serve garnished with lime wedges and fresh coriander (cilantro).

MONKFISH

Monkfish is a very meaty fish, resembling lobster, which could be used instead of monkfish for a special occasion.

CHAPTER FIVE

Vegetables & Rice

Vegetables are rarely eaten on their own because northern Pakistan is very much a meat-eating country. Instead, they are used in meat dishes to make a complete meal in one dish, or made into tasty accompanying dishes, often cooked in a typical tomato, onion, garam masala and fresh coriander (cilantro) sauce, or stir-fried with freshly ground spices. These vegetable dishes make wonderful vegetarian meals and most Balti curry houses will serve a wide selection of either vegetarian dishes or side dishes of vegetables.

Any combination of vegetables can be used in the following recipes. Pulses are widely used and can be bought either dried or canned, in health food stores, supermarkets or Asian food stores.

Vegetables have a long history of being sun-dried for use in the cold winter months in northern Pakistan. I have included two rice dishes because, although authentically naan bread or chapatis should be eaten with a Balti curry, some people prefer rice.

Opposite: *Steep mountainsides in the Hunza valley are built into narrow terraced fields, ideal for growing crops like rice.*

STEP 1

STEP 2

STEP 3

STEP 4

MUSTARD & ONION POTATOES

Mustard seeds give the potatoes a nutty taste. This dish can be served with any type of cuisine, not just curry, and is good served with barbecued koftas in the summer.

SERVES 4
PREPARATION: 10 MINS,
   COOKING: 20–25 MINS

350 g/12 oz small new potatoes
3 tbsp oil
2 tbsp brown mustard seeds
1 tsp cumin seeds
1 tsp crushed dried red chillies
250 g/8 oz baby onions
1 garlic clove, chopped
1 cm/1/2 inch piece ginger root
1/4 tsp Garam Masala (see page 78)

1 Boil the potatoes in salted water for 10–15 minutes until just tender. Drain the potatoes, cut in half if they are on the largish side, and set aside.

2 Heat the oil in a Balti pan or wok, add the mustard seeds, cumin, and chillies and fry until the seeds start popping.

3 Add the onions to the pan and stir-fry until golden brown. Add the garlic and ginger and fry for 1 minute.

4 Stir in the potatoes and garam masala and stir-fry for 4–5 minutes until the potatoes are golden brown. Serve hot.

VARIATIONS

This recipe can be made with any combination of vegetable to make a tasty dry stir-fry dish, to go with any of the curries in this book. One of my favourites is to substitute the new potatoes with the sweet variety. These make a wonderful potato salad if served cold and are ideal with barbecues in the summer. If you like a moist potato salad add 3 tbsp of yogurt stirred into the potatoes. You could also add 1 tbsp of chopped mint to the yogurt.

STEP 1

STEP 2

STEP 3

STEP 4

SWEET POTATOES & SPINACH

Sweet potatoes are similar to the sweet, waxy potatoes that are grown in the mountainous regions of Asia.

SERVES 4
PREPARATION: 10 MINS,
   COOKING: 15 MINS

500 g/1lb sweet potatoes, cut into 2.5 cm/
   1 inch cubes
4 tbsp oil
2 onions, sliced
1 garlic clove, crushed
125 g/4 oz/1 cup pine nuts, toasted
500 g/1 lb fresh spinach
1 tsp Garam Masala (see page 78)
2 tbsp chopped dried red chillies
2 tsp water
freshly grated nutmeg to serve

1 Boil the sweet potatoes in salted water for 5 minutes until half cooked. Drain and set aside.

2 Heat the oil in a Balti pan or wok, add the onions and stir-fry until golden brown.

3 Add the garlic, sweet potatoes and pine nuts to the pan and stir-fry for 2 minutes until the sweet potatoes have absorbed the oil.

4 Stir in the spinach, garam masala and dried chillies and stir-fry for 2 minutes. Add the water and stir-fry for 4 minutes until the sweet potatoes and spinach are tender.

5 Serve with freshly grated nutmeg sprinkled over.

QUICK TIP

Fresh spinach can be substituted with 1kg/ 2 lb of frozen leaf spinach. Fresh chillies can be used instead of dried chilles if you do not have any.

SWEET POTATOES

Sweet potatoes are longer than ordinary potatoes and have a pinkish or yellowish skin with yellow or white flesh. As their name suggests, they taste slightly sweet.

MIXED VEGETABLE BALTI

Any combination of vegetables or pulses can be used in this recipe. It would make a good dish to serve to your vegetarian friends or with one of the meat or fish dishes.

STEP 1

STEP 2

STEP 3

STEP 4

SERVES 4
PREPARATION: 20 MINS,
  COOKING: 55 MINS

250 g/8 oz/1 cup split yellow peas, washed
3 tbsp oil
1 tsp onion seeds
2 onions, sliced
125 g/4 oz courgettes (zucchini), sliced
125 g/4 oz potatoes, cut into 1 cm/¹/₂ inch cubes
125 g/4 oz carrots, sliced
1 small aubergine (eggplant), sliced
250 g/8 oz tomatoes, chopped
300 ml/¹/₂ pint/1¹/₄ cups water
3 garlic cloves, chopped
1 tsp ground cumin
1 tsp ground coriander
1 tsp salt
2 fresh green chillies, sliced
¹/₂ tsp Garam Masala (see page 78)
2 tbsp chopped fresh coriander (cilantro)

1 Put the split peas into a saucepan and cover with salted water. Bring to the boil and simmer for 30 minutes. Drain the peas and keep warm.

2 Heat the oil in a Balti pan or wok, add the onion seeds and fry until they start popping. Add the onions and stir-fry until golden brown.

3 Add the courgettes (zucchini), potatoes, carrots and aubergine (eggplant) to the pan and stir-fry for 2 minutes.

4 Stir in the tomatoes, water, garlic, cumin, ground coriander, salt, chillies, garam masala and reserved split peas. Bring to the boil, then simmer for 15 minutes until all the vegetables are tender. Stir the fresh coriander (cilantro) into the vegetables and serve.

T I P

The split peas can be cooked in the Balti pan or wok. After draining the split peas, remove them and keep them warm, wipe out the pan out and continue with steps 2–4.

STEP 1

STEP 2

STEP 3

STEP 4

BALTI DAL

Chang dal is the husked, split, black chick-pea (garbanzo bean), which is yellow on the inside and has a nutty taste. Throughout Pakistan and India dal is eaten as a side dish with most curries.

SERVES 4
PREPARATION: 8 MINS,
   COOKING: 1 HR 10 MINS

250 g/8 oz/1 cup chang dal or split yellow
  peas, washed
$^1/_2$ tsp ground turmeric
1 tsp ground coriander
1 tsp salt
4 curry leaves
2 tbsp oil
$^1/_2$ tsp asafoetida powder (optional)
1 tsp cumin seeds
2 onions, chopped
2 garlic cloves, crushed
1 cm/$^1/_2$ inch piece ginger root, grated
$^1/_2$ tsp Garam Masala (see page 78)

1 Put the chang dal in a saucepan and pour in enough water to cover by 2.5 cm/1 inch. Bring to the boil and spoon off the scum that has formed.

2 Add the turmeric, ground coriander, salt and curry leaves and simmer for 1 hour. The chang dal should be tender, but not mushy.

3 Heat the oil in a Balti pan or wok, add the asafoetida, if using, and fry for 30 seconds. Add the cumin seeds and fry until they start popping. Add the onions and stir-fry until golden brown.

4 Add the garlic, ginger, garam masala and chang dal and stir-fry for 2 minutes. Serve hot with one of the Balti curries.

DAL

Dal reheats and keeps well, so it is a good idea to make a large amount and store in the refrigerator, or freeze in portions.

PUMPKIN KORMA

*Korma is one of the most popular curries worldwide and in Pakistan
each region has its own version.*

STEP 1

SERVES 4
PREPARATION: 15 MINS,
  COOKING: 20–25 MINS

4 tbsp oil
¹/₂ tsp onion seeds
4 curry leaves
2 onions, chopped
500 g/1 lb peeled and deseeded pumpkin, cut
  into 2.5 cm/1 inch cubes
150 ml/¹/₄ pint/²/₃ cup natural yogurt
1 cm/¹/₂ inch piece ginger root, grated
2 garlic cloves, crushed
125 g/4 oz/1 cup ground almonds
¹/₂ tsp ground turmeric
¹/₂ tsp chilli powder
¹/₂ tsp Garam Masala (see page 78)
1 tsp salt
150 ml/¹/₄ pint/²/₃ cup coconut milk
1 tbsp chopped fresh coriander (cilantro)

TO GARNISH:
1 tbsp chopped toasted almonds
1 tbsp chopped fresh coriander (cilantro)

1 Heat the oil in a Balti pan or wok,
add the onion seeds and curry
leaves and fry until the seeds start
popping.

2 Add the onions to the pan and stir-
fry until golden brown.

3 Stir in the pumpkin and stir-fry
until golden brown.

4 Stir in the yogurt gradually to
prevent it curdling. Add the ginger,
garlic, almonds, turmeric, chilli powder,
garam masala, salt, coconut milk and
fresh coriander (cilantro) and simmer for
10–15 minutes until the pumpkin is
tender. Serve garnished with toasted
almonds and fresh coriander (cilantro).

STEP 2

STEP 3

PUMPKIN

There are many varieties of pumpkin
available in supermarkets. It is not only
the flesh of the pumpkin that is used in
cooking but also the seeds. If these are
toasted, they make a nutty topping to
vegetables. Pumpkin seeds are left to dry
on the balconies and roofs of the houses
in Pakistan.

STEP 4

STEP 1: Aromatic Rice

STEP 2: Aromatic Rice

STEP 1: Saffron Rice

STEP 2: Saffron Rice

AROMATIC BASMATI RICE & SPICY SAFFRON RICE

For the best results when cooking rice it is important to remove the starch before cooking, by rinsing the raw rice under the tap and then soaking it in cold water for 30 minutes

SERVES 4
PREPARATION: 10 MINS,
  SOAKING: 30 MINS,
  COOKING: 20–25 MINS

AROMATIC BASMATI RICE

1 tbsp oil
1 cinnamon stick
2 dried bay leaves
4 green cardamom pods
4 black peppercorns
250 g/8 oz/1 cup basmati rice, washed and
  soaked
1 tsp salt

1 Heat the oil in a heavy-based saucepan and fry the cinnamon, bay leaves, cardamom pods and black peppercorns for 30 seconds.

2 Add the rice and salt and enough water to cover the rice by 2.5 cm/1 inch. Cover with a tight-fitting lid, bring to the boil and simmer for 20 minutes or until all the water has been absorbed and the rice is tender.

SPICY SAFFRON RICE

60 g/2 oz/¼ cup butter or ghee
1 onion, chopped
½ tsp saffron strands
1 tsp cumin seeds
250 g/8 oz/1 cup basmati rice, washed and
  soaked
1 tsp salt
90 g/3 oz/⅔ cup split almonds, ¾ cut in
  slivers and toasted

1 Heat the butter or ghee in a heavy-based saucepan, add the onion and stir-fry. Add the saffron strands and cumin seeds and fry for 30 seconds.

2 Add the rice and fry for 2 minutes until it has absorbed the oil and the saffron colour. Add the salt and enough water to cover the rice by 2.5 cm/1 inch. Cover with a tight-fitting lid and simmer for 20 minutes until all the water has been absorbed and the rice is tender. Stir in the almonds.

PLAIN BOILED RICE

Cook the rice in the same way as the aromatic basmati rice, omitting the spices.

BALTI COOKING

SPICES USED IN BALTI COOKING

Spices are an essential part of Balti cooking.

Asafoetida

Asafoetida comes from the stem and root of the giant fennel. It has a rather nauseating smell but this disappears in cooking, and only a small amount should be used. Asafoetida is available in block or powder form, and you will probably find it only in Asian food stores. The powder is more convenient to use. Both forms must be kept in a well-sealed jar so as not to smell out your spice cupboard.

Cardamom

Cardamom grows as a pod, which is white (bleached), green or black; the best ones to use are the green pods, which are also the most common. The pods can be used whole, or they can be crushed and the small black seeds inside can be extracted and used whole or ground.

Coriander (cilantro)

Fresh coriander (cilantro) is one of the main ingredients in Balti cooking and the majority of the recipes will have fresh coriander (cilantro) stirred in or sprinkled over the cooked dish. Fresh coriander (cilantro) has quite a pungent taste, and is sold in bunches, rather like fresh parsley.

Balti cooking developed in mountainous areas of northern Pakistan, where there is a region called Baltistan. The translation of Balti literally means 'cooking bucket', which refers to the traditional Pakistani deep, two-handled cooking pot with a rounded bottom. Balti curries are quick to cook using the stir-fry method, and can be served in the traditional cooking pot. They typically use ground or whole spices and fresh coriander (cilantro).

Pakistan borders India, China, Afghanistan and Iran, so its cuisine has been subject to a varied cross-section of influences throughout the centuries. For example, the Balti pan has arguably developed from the Chinese wok. The Moguls have also played a part in influencing the food and cooking of northern Pakistan; they spent the hot summer months in the cool hills of Kashmir, bringing with them new recipes, foods and spices. Spices were traded on the silk route from China and made their way down into Pakistan over the Karakoram mountains, on their way to India. Spices were a vital link in overland trading, which in itself was a far more treacherous method of transport than the later sea routes.

Balti curries are traditionally eaten with naan bread or chapatis, instead of rice. The naan bread or chapati is used to scoop up the sauce and meat, straight from the Balti pan in which it is served; this is how you will find it served in authentic Balti curry houses. Naan bread and chapatis can be bought in Asian food stores and most supermarkets, and are best served warm.

One of the great things about Balti curries is that you can mix and match them, and add your own choice of ingredients. This is particularly the case with spices, so you can alter the curry to suit your particular tastes. The heat of the curry can be altered depending whether you like a hot, fiery curry or a milder, spicy one. Chillies, whether they are powdered, dried or fresh, are one of the main hot ingredients, and should be used with caution until you discover just how hot you like your curry. If your guests' spice tolerance differs, the best policy is to divide the curry during the final stages of cooking and add dried chillies or extra garam masala as appropriate.

EQUIPMENT

Most well equipped kitchens will have the necessary equipment for cooking Balti curries, such as good heavy-based saucepans with tight-fitting lids, sharp knives, a chopping board, sieves (strainers) and spoons. However, there are a few items which could prove useful and time saving:

Balti pan

The main item you will need is a Balti pan or a good quality wok. A Balti pan, or Karahi, is the traditional cooking pan used throughout Pakistan and India. It is a real all-purpose pan, as it is used for stir-frying, deep-frying and slow simmering. Originally, the pans were made of cast iron and had a rounded base, but now they come in a variety of metals and, in order to fit modern cookers, have a flattened base. A Balti pan or wok should always be heated before the oil or spices are added.

A new pan needs to be seasoned before it is used for cooking for the first time. To do this, wash the pan, then heat some oil until nearly smoking; maintain this temperature for 10 minutes, making sure you swirl the oil carefully around the insides of the pan. Discard the oil and wipe out the pan with paper towels; it is now ready to use. To clean a Balti pan it is best to use a bamboo wok-cleaning brush.

Electric coffee grinder or spice mill

Either an electric coffee grinder or spice mill will greatly cut down the time taken to grind the spices. If using a coffee grinder that is also used for coffee, always remember to clean the grinder thoroughly afterwards, otherwise you will end up with strange tasting coffee, or coffee-tasting curries.

If you don't have either an electric coffee grinder or spice mill, use a pestle and mortar, which will take longer and is not so good for finely ground spices or large quantities.

Food processor or blender

A food processor or blender will really help to save time in the preparation of a Balti curry because they are able to purée, chop and grate ingredients more quickly and with far less effort than doing these tasks manually.

A food processor or blender will also grind spices, but not as finely as a coffee grinder or spice mill, and it is not very good for small quantities.

BALTI INGREDIENTS

Most of the ingredients needed for Balti cooking can be found in supermarkets, which now have a large range of different foods from around the world. If there are any ingredients that you cannot find in a supermarket, visit a specialist Asian store. Many of the special ingredients can be substituted, or you can make up your own combination using the spices you have and the recipes as a guide.

Meat, poultry, fish and vegetables should be cut into bite-size pieces to make them quicker to cook and easier to scoop up with naan bread. It is best to use good quality ingredients in Balti cooking. Balti dishes are only cooked for a short time, so the dishes will only be as good as the ingredients used.

Fat is an essential part of a Balti curry, and traditionally ghee is used. Ghee is clarified butter and gives a much richer taste to a curry than ordinary butter or oil. However, many people today are health-conscious, so may prefer to use vegetable oil or corn oil.

Whole spices, such as whole curry leaves, bay leaves, cinnamon sticks, cloves, cardamom pods and black peppercorns, are fried in oil to release their flavour and aroma. They should not be eaten.

Coriander seeds

Coriander seeds are light brown and very aromatic; they are used whole or crushed. Coriander seeds can also be bought ground.

Curry leaves

Curry leaves are similar to bay leaves but are smaller and thinner, with a spicy aroma and flavour. They can be found in Asian food stores. Alternatively, use bay leaves.

Fenugreek

Both the leaves and seeds of fenugreek are used, but the stalks and root should be discarded, as they have a bitter taste. Fresh fenugreek is sold in bunches, like parsley and fresh coriander (cilantro). Fenugreek seeds are flat and yellowish brown in colour. Ground fenugreek is used in commercially produced curry powders.

Garlic

Crushed or chopped garlic is used in most Balti dishes. You can purée garlic and freeze it in portions in an ice cube tray to save time preparing individual dishes. To purée garlic, work it in a food processor or blender until it forms a fine paste, or pound it in a pestle and mortar; in either case, you may need to add a small quantity of water to form a purée.

Ginger

Fresh ginger root looks rather like a knobbly potato. The skin should be peeled, then the flesh either grated, chopped or sliced. Ginger is also available ground; this can be used as a substitute for fresh root ginger, but the fresh root is far superior; use 1 teaspoon ground ginger to each 1 cm/ ½ inch piece ginger root.

Mustard seeds

These small round seeds can be white, black, or brown; the last are the ones used most often in Balti dishes. Mustard seeds should be fried in hot oil to extract their flavour.

Onion seeds

Onion seeds are small and black. They may be labelled as *kalonj* in Asian food stores. Onion seeds can be used instead of pepper, but have a spicier and more bitter taste.

Pomegranate seeds

You will probably find tangy, fruity tasting dried pomegranate seeds only in Asian food stores. If you cannot find dried seeds, you can use fresh pomegranate seeds.

Poppy seeds

Small, hard poppy seeds can be black or white; white are used most often in Balti cooking. Poppy seeds are usually roasted or fried in oil, then used whole or ground. When ground, they also act as a thickening agent.

Garam Masala

Garam masala means 'hot mixed' and will be needed for most of the recipes. It is a good idea to make a batch and store it in an airtight container for no longer than 3 months. Then you will have fresh garam masala available whenever you come to cook a Balti curry.

Ready-prepared garam masala can be bought in supermarkets and Asian food stores. This is the recipe I have used, but you can alter it to suit your own taste.

3 cm/ 1¹/₄ inch piece cinnamon stick
³/₄ tsp black peppercorns
8 green cardamom pods
1 tsp cloves
1 tsp cumin seeds
1 tsp coriander seeds
¹/₂ small nutmeg

1. Heat a dry Balti pan or heavy frying pan (skillet), add the spices and roast until they have darkened slightly. Alternatively, roast the spices in a preheated oven at 180°C/350°F/Gas mark 4 for 5 minutes until they turn a slightly darker colour. Leave to cool.

2. Put the roast spices into a coffee grinder, spice mill or pestle and mortar, and grind to a fine powder. Use straight away or store for later use.

Par-cooked Balti meat

Balti dishes are stir-fried so it is necessary to cook tougher cuts of meat, such as braising steak, beforehand. If you don't want to do this, you will have to cook the Balti curry for about 1 hour, preferably in a covered dish in a preheated oven at 180°C/350°F/Gas mark 4. Here is a recipe for par-cooked meat.

Par-cooked lamb or beef

1 tbsp oil
250 g/8 oz/2 cups chopped onion
2 garlic cloves, crushed
1 tsp ground ginger
1 fresh green chilli, chopped
1 tsp Garam Masala
1 tbsp tomato purée (paste)
1 tsp salt
¹/₂ tsp brown onion seeds
200 ml/7 fl oz/1 scant cup water
750 g/1¹/₂ lb braising steak or lamb, cubed

1. Heat the oil in a flameproof casserole, add the onion and fry until softened. Add the garlic and fry for 1 minute.

2. Stir in the remaining ingredients and bring to the boil. Put the lid on the casserole and cook in a preheated oven at 200°C/400°F/Gas mark 6, allowing 40 minutes for lamb and 1 hour for beef. The meat should be tender but still pink in the centre. Remove the meat with a perforated spoon and keep the contents of the casserole to make a Balti sauce.

Balti sauce

The sauce from the par-cooked meat is used to add extra liquid and flavour to some of the recipes. To make the sauce, put all the ingredients into a food processor or blender and blend to a smooth purée. Alternatively, push the ingredients through a sieve (strainer). It is a good idea is to make double the quantity of sauce and freeze it in portions. Use the sauce as required in a recipe or add it to any of the curries that need a little extra liquid.

A vegetarian Balti sauce can be made by omitting the meat from the par-cooked meat recipe; cook the sauce in the oven or on the hob for 40 minutes.

If you don't have time to make the sauce, use stock to replace it in a recipe.

BALTI CURRY PREPARATION

Adding the ingredients in quick succession is very much a part of Balti cooking, so before you start to cook a curry, have all the ingredients ready and the spices roasted and ground, if necessary.

The ingredient list may look long on some of the recipes, but don't be put off, as most of the ingredients are spices so do not take a lot of preparation.

Marinating
Meat, poultry, fish and seafood can all be marinated to give them a wonderful flavour. Where marinating is called for in the recipes, it should be done after grinding the spices. All the marinade ingredients should be mixed together in a bowl, the meat, poultry, fish or seafood stirred in, then the bowl covered and left in the refrigerator to marinate, ideally overnight. Marinating needs a bit of forward planning, but if you don't have time to leave it overnight, leave it for a minimum of 1 hour.

Stir-frying
Stir-frying for Balti cooking can be done in a Balti pan or wok. The pan should be heated before you add the oil. The oil should be heated over a high heat before the food is added. This is usually cooked over high heat, and is kept on the move, to ensure it does not stick. Then the heat can be turned down to cook the food as required for the rest of the recipe.

SPICES

The best spices to buy are whole spices, as they will keep for much longer than ground spices. If you do buy ground, purchase small quantities at a time. A wide selection of spices can be found in the supermarkets and the more unusual ones can be bought from specialist Asian food stores. It is best to store spices in airtight containers in a cool cupboard, rather than in a spice rack in the kitchen, because light and warmth will affect the colour and freshness. A good idea is to have racks on the inside of a cupboard door, so you can find the spices easily.

Freshly ground spices have a stronger aroma and flavour than bought ground spices. Store ground spices in an airtight container. No ground spice should be stored for longer than 3 months.

Roasting spices
Roasting brings out the flavour of spices, but be careful not to burn them. The spices can be roasted in a preheated oven at 180°C/350°F/Gas mark 4 for 5 minutes until they turn a slightly darker colour, but the easiest way to roast them is to dry-fry them in a Balti pan or heavy-based frying pan (skillet). Heat the pan then add the spices and cook for 2–5 minutes, depending on the quantity, until they have darkened slightly.

Saffron
Saffron strands are the yellowish orange stigmas of the saffron crocus. The strands have a pungent aroma and bittersweet taste. Saffron is one of the world's most expensive spices, as it takes about 200,000–300,000 stigmas to produce 500 g/1 lb of dried saffron strands, but it takes only a small quantity to flavour and colour a dish. Saffron strands should be a dark orange colour and can be bought in small jars or packets. The strands should be fried, or soaked in milk or water, before being added to a dish.

Tamarind
Tamarind comes from the bean-shaped pod of the tamarind tree and can be bought as a paste, or as a block, which needs to be soaked. Tamarind has a sour taste similar to lemon juice so you could use 1 tablespoon of lemon juice to replace 30 g/ 1 oz of tamarind block or paste.

Turmeric
Tumeric comes from the root of a gingerlike plant, and is usually sold ground and dried. Turmeric is bright yellow and will colour food yellow, so can be used as a cheaper colouring agent than saffron, but the flavour is very different. Turmeric is used in commercially prepared curry powders and gives them their typical yellow colour.

INDEX